MUSLIMS AND CHRISTIANS:
ENEMIES OR BROTHERS?

JEAN-RENE MILOT

MUSLIMS AND CHRISTIANS:
Enemies or Brothers?

Translated by
SR. MARY THOMAS NOBLE, OP

ALBA·HOUSE   NEW·YORK
SOCIETY OF ST. PAUL, 2187 VICTORY BLVD., STATEN ISLAND, NEW YORK 10314

ST PAULS

Originally published in French by Médiaspaul (Montreal, Canada: 1995) under the title: *Musulmans et chrétiens: des frères ennemis?* Cover illustrations: Details of two miniatures from the 14th century courtesy of Médiaspaul.

Library of Congress Cataloging-in-Publication Data

Milot, Jean-René.
   [Musulmans et chrétiens. English]
   Muslims and Christians: enemies or brothers? / Jean-René Milot: translated by Mary Thomas Noble.
     p.   cm.
   Originally published: Montreal: Médiaspaul, 1995 under the title: Musulmans et chrétiens: des frères ennemis?
   Includes bibliographical references.
   ISBN: 0-8189-0779-7
   1. Islam — Relations — Christianity. 2. Christianity and other religions — Islam. I. Title.
BP172.M8713   1997
261.2'7 — dc20   96-36972
                                        CIP

Produced and designed in the United States of America by the Fathers and Brothers of the Society of St. Paul,
2187 Victory Boulevard, Staten Island, New York 10314,
as part of their communications apostolate.

ISBN: 0-8189-0779-7

This edition simultaneously published in 1997
and distributed in the Philippines by

ST PAULS
7708 St. Paul Rd., SAV, Makati City
1203 Metro Manila, Philippines
Tel. 895-9701 to 04; Fax (632) 890-7131

Philippines ISBN: 971-504-599-5

ST PAULS is an apostolate of the priests and brothers of the Society of St. Paul who proclaim the Gospel through the media of social communication.

Printing Information:

Current Printing - first digit   1   2   3   4   5   6   7   8   9   10

Year of Current Printing - first year shown

1997   1998   1999   2000   2001   2002   2003

Table of Contents

Muslims and Christians:
Enemies or Brothers?

"Christians versus Moslems" — "the cross versus the crescent" — "Christianity versus Islam": too often in recent years these concepts have been paired in connection with political conflicts, military confrontations, or socio-ethnic tensions. The monotonous refrain has created the impression that Christianity and Islam are fierce antagonists whose only object is to tear each other to pieces.

In many instances this impression seems partially confirmed and validated by the inflammatory declarations of certain religious or political leaders. If we were to believe their rhetoric with its demagogic overtones, Christianity and Islam are engaged in a fight to the death for domination of the world. More or less consciously, the media have become accomplices in this propaganda which has generated fear and mistrust if not downright hatred. The climate thus created gives rise to further tensions.

This mounting irruption could blind us to a whole sector of reality and distort our sense of proportion in regard to the current situation. The pages which follow make no claim to arbitrate secular conflicts or to propose miraculous solutions for current tensions. The situation we now know is in part the result of several centuries of history, particularly the more recent history of the colonial venture and its consequences. We cannot reshape history, nor can we bring about instantaneous changes in the status quo.

But it is always possible to try to identify the traditional religious roots of these tensions, with an eye to the shared religious patrimony of Islam and Christianity. By focussing our attention on the specific differing characteristics of each of these great religions, we often lose sight of what they have in common, which is perhaps far more considerable than what distinguishes them.

Furthermore, in situating Christianity and Islam within the context of the modern world, we can observe certain distinctions in their respective ways of responding to the challenges of modernity. But here again, we may wonder whether the positions of Christians and Muslims are not very similar, both as believers and, perhaps more basically, as human beings.

This is the approach to which the reader is invited: a step back from daily affairs, an openness to "the other," a weighing of current impressions and a reflection on some less obvious but perhaps more basic facts. Doubtless this will not produce a change in immediate realities, but it may modify our perceptions.

Our Common
Religious Patrimony

Common roots

Muslims, Christians and Jews all claim Abraham as their ancestor in the faith. For these believers, what differentiated Abraham from his contemporaries was that he adored only one deity, a unique and personal deity who entered into a relationship with him. This deity the Jews name Yahweh. Christians call him God, and Muslims, Allah. In the eyes of these believers, however, there is but one and the same deity, the God of Abraham.

For Muslims, Abraham (in Arabic, *Ibrahim*) is the founder of the sanctuary of Mecca. It is he who received from heaven, by way of a sign, the black stone which Muslims venerate in the cube-shaped enclosure of the Kaaba when they go on pilgrimage to Mecca. In fact most of the pilgrimage rites (*hadj* or *hajj*) are enriched with memories of Abraham. They celebrate various events in his life with which the faithful identify in intention. For example, the sacrifice of a lamb, with which Muslims throughout the world associate themselves at the time of the "Great Feast" ('*Eid al-Adbâ*), recalls the sacrifice of Abraham. At the moment when he prepared to immolate his son, Allah sent an angel to substitute a ram for the sacrifice. This son, in Muslim tradition, is Ishmael, ancestor of the Arabs, the son of Hagar, Abraham's slave girl. When she went out into the desert with her son to die, Allah answered Hagar's prayer by causing water to spring up. This became the sacred well of Zemzem; pilgrims sprinkle themselves with its water.

For Muslims as for Christians, the God of Abraham spoke to men and sent them prophets or messengers. From the viewpoint of the Quran, the sacred book of the Muslims, Adam was the first of the prophets, the one to whom Allah revealed all that a man needed to know in order to lead a good life in this world, from the moment of his creation until the time when Allah would bring him back to himself. At this point he would be rewarded with heaven or punished with hell, depending upon whether or not he had conformed to Allah's expectations.

As we read in Bible history, men forgot what the prophets had said, and Allah in his great goodness sent more prophets periodically to remind them of his message. The message remained fundamentally the same; each prophet simply repeated it for those to whom he was sent. According to the tenets of Islam, certain prophets were the bearers of a Book: Moses transmitted the Torah, David the Psalms, and Jesus the Gospels. Finally Muhammad, the last of the prophets, transmitted the Quran, the last Book which seals off revelation.

According to the Quran, Jesus is a very great prophet. In a moving way it[1] recounts the prodigies surrounding his virgin birth, and the miracles he worked. Myriam (Mary) is the only feminine proper name to be found in the Quran.

The Quran is "a book of warning." Like the Bible, it challenges men's actions and reminds them of how they should behave toward God and their fellow men: submission and confidence are to be shown to Allah; justice, compassion and generosity to men. Among other things daily prayer, fasting, and almsgiving are prescribed for believers. Here we have attitudes common to both Christians and Muslims.

---

[1] Quran, s. 19, v. 1726. The Gospel, according to the Quran, is revealed to Jesus: "And in their footsteps We sent Jesus the son of Mary, confirming the Law that had come before him: We sent him the Gospel: therein was guidance and light, and confirmation of the Law that had come before him... (v. 49). Christians are the people of the Book" (v. 62).

Doctrinal differences

In a general way we could say that, of all sacred books, the Quran is closest to the Christians' Bible. There are, however, many differences in content between the two books, and substantial doctrinal differences between Christians and Muslims. These differences bear chiefly on the person of Jesus and the question of the Trinity.

For the Quran, Jesus is "the son of Mary" but not "the Son of God." He is not the Incarnate God, the Word made flesh. He was not crucified: someone else was substituted for him. He will rise at the end of time to summon men to judgment.

To a devout Muslim, if Allah is one and unique he can have neither son nor equal. And if Christians believe that God is "triune," that he has a Son, that this Son became incarnate, was crucified, and has already arisen, Muslims believe they have not understood the Scriptures well, or have falsified them. For Christians, this last affirmation might seem, at the very least, gratuitous. For Muslims it is in reality a logical enough conclusion, flowing from the premises of the Quran: the Quran is the final recalling of previous revelations; its message is the eternal message of Allah to mankind, which he entrusted to the preceding prophets, including Jesus. If Christians, therefore, on hearing the Quran proclaimed by the Prophet Muhammad at Mecca and at Medina, have not recognized this message, it is because they have misunderstood their own Scriptures or falsified them, suppressing among other things the prophecy announcing the coming of Ahmad (Muhammad).

Logically enough, too, Christians have responded to this affirmation by contesting the premises. Taking their stand similarly upon their own beliefs, they have challenged the revealed character of the Quran and the mission of the Prophet. Since for them it is the New Testament which puts the final seal upon revelation, Muhammad could not be a true prophet nor could the Quran be a true revelation. On the basis of this conviction the medieval Christian was to fabricate a legend which would serve the cause of the Crusades very well. According to this legend Muhammad was in reality a person called Mahon, a heretical imposter who, under the inspiration of Satan, passed for a prophet by inventing revelations according to the needs of the moment, in order to satisfy his lowest instincts.[2]

---

[2] This, to a Muslim, is nothing short of blasphemy and the reason for the condemnation by many of Salman Rushdie, whose central character in his novel *Satanic Verses* is Mahon.

One might think that this sort of polemics concerning Jesus and Muhammad was the cause of the Crusades, those military attempts of Christians to conquer the Holy Land and to "deliver the land of Jesus" from the control of the Muslims. In reality, the opposite was true. The motives behind the Crusades were primarily political and economic. In order to channel the frustrated energies of warriors and keep them occupied with something other than the pillaging of Europe and mutual slaughter, what could be more useful than a common enemy living at the end of the world? In a period when religious sentiment permeated society, to invoke religious reasons was to legitimize the Crusades and to mobilize, behind the standard of the faith, subjects who would otherwise be recalcitrant and unruly.

Above all it would be a mistake to think that throughout this period only the Crusades figured heavily in the relationship between Christians and Muslims.[3] These limited and local confrontations

---

[3] During the 8th century, for example, there were some Christians who had very close contact with Muslim Caliphs, for example, St. John Damascene (d. 749 AD). He was a minister at the court of the Umayyads. He enjoyed many personal contacts with Muslims and had a profound respect for Islam which is important in any kind of dialogue. In the 13th century St. Francis of Assisi visited the Muslim Sultan in Egypt to start a peaceful

did not prevent the free circulation of culture and civilization, as we shall see further on. Nor did they prevent the growth of two great mystical traditions which had too much in common to be developed in complete isolation from one another.

Mystical parallels

Undoubtedly it is on the mystical level that Islam and Christianity find most points of convergence. Biographers of the Prophet Muhammad mention the presence of Christian monks in the desert. The Quran[4] has some helpful contributions on the subject. According to tradition Muhammad encountered Christian monks in the course of his travels by caravan and even talked with one of

---

dialogue with him. He also wanted to establish his fraternities there. Impressed by the Muslims' call to prayer, he encouraged his friars to ring church bells to announce the hours for services. In the same century, the Dominican friars made many efforts to dialogue with Muslims and for this purpose they established study centers in Tunis in 1250. There were good relations with Muslims which made it possible to learn Arabic and Islamic culture in the Muslim city. Later such centers were also established in Barcelona and Valencia (James Channan, O.P., *Christian-Muslim Dialogue in Pakistan*, Lahore, National Commission for Christian-Muslim Relations, 1995).

[4] Quran, s. 5, v. 82.

them, the monk Bahira. Soon, in Islam, while the armies of the caliphs were subjugating vast regions, devout Muslims were fleeing the power, splendor, and wealth of the courts to devote themselves to meditation and fasting. Theirs was the same reaction as that of the Christian monks of the East, the desert Fathers, a few centuries earlier.

Little by little these devout Muslims gathered into groups and formed schools for the disciples who joined them. It is interesting to note among their practices the technique of meditation centered upon the repetition of the divine name, harmonized with the rhythm of breathing. This recalls the "Jesus prayer," a practice of Eastern Christian mystics at the heart of hesychasm (a quality of interior stillness or silence in which one listens to God and communicates with him from the heart).

Reaching maturity, so to speak, in the tenth and eleventh centuries, Muslim mysticism, called "Sufism," produced lengthy treatises describing the mystical pilgrimage, the journey of the soul enamored of God, from his entrance into the way through asceticism and the stripping of self in confident abandonment to God, to illumination, when the mystic was ravished out of himself at the highest point of his mind and heart, to lose himself in the Other. This was ecstasy. The mystic was said to "disappear" in some way from himself and to "survive" in God, the object of his search and his love. He retained consciousness of himself only insofar as was necessary to survive as a distinct individual.

This journey of the Sufi guided by his master is described as a succession of gradual stages called "states" or "stations" whose elements have been analyzed with remarkable psychological acumen. Some centuries later in a Spain where there were still Muslims, Teresa of Avila and John of the Cross dreamed, as children, of going to cross swords with them (they were then called Saracens or Moors), for the greater glory of God. Later the two would emulate the great Muslim mystics in waging war against their own desires so as to make room for God. Is it pure coincidence that they described the journey toward God in images such as "The Ascent of Mount Carmel" and "The Interior Castle"? The least we can say is that the experiences they describe seem to be basically the same as those of the great Muslim mystics and the Christian mystics of the East.

As was the case with Christianity, so too the mystical movement in Islam gave rise to religious Orders dedicated to the search for God through the observance of a rule left by a holy founder. These Orders gradually drew masses of believers and proposed to them practices such as the recitation of "the ninety-nine most beautiful names of Allah"[5] which appear in the Quran. In order to do this they were given a memory aid, a cord with knots similar to the rosary which St. Dominic gave to Christians. The Sufi monasteries, like those in Europe, were centers of culture and civilization, sanctuaries from barbarian invasions or the despotism of certain rulers.

Just as in Europe, groups similar to the Third Orders were formed in the neighborhood of the Sufi monasteries, giving rise to guilds of artisans grouped around patron saints. Gradually the activity of the Sufis left the orbit of the mysticism of the "classical" period to enter that of popular religion. For many believers the cult of the saints competed with strict faith in one God. In lending supernatural powers to human beings, some felt that they were making them rivals of God. In Islam as in Christianity there would be reactions to these abuses, especially in the modern period.

---

[5] Descriptive Arabic expressions which present Allah as the One who listens, sees, gives, remembers, forgives, protects, guides, etc.

If Islam and Christianity are so close to one another at the mystical level,[6] this may perhaps be because mystics yearn to go to God directly by the shortest road, that of contemplation. They seek a face to face encounter, without the encumbrance of professions of faith, intellectual concepts, and doctrines. In a certain way their experience is sufficient in itself; it does not need to be validated by reasonings and explanations, or by an authority outside of the mystical way. What confirms their experience for them is the intuitive and intimate knowledge of a unique Absolute, whose features transcend confessional differences and the relative categories men use in attempting to describe Him.

---

[6] In the 20th century Professor Louis Massignon contributed a great deal to modern Christian-Muslim dialogue precisely through his intimate knowledge of Islamic mysticism. He, in fact, discovered his Catholic faith through the works of a great Muslim mystic al-Hallaj. He devoted 50 years to a study of this mystic and made the richness of Islamic civilization known to the West. His research made him realize how close Muslim and Christian mystics are, particularly when contemplatives on both sides leave the exterior form of piety and reach interior communion with God.

Belief and doctrine, faith and theology

In the measure in which the believer's religious experience approximates that of the mystic, we are led to view the differences between Christians and Muslims from a new perspective which suggests that these differences are found at the level of doctrine rather than faith. Actually, faith — the act of believing — is quite simple when it first arises in the heart of the believer. It is a kind of acquiescence to an Absolute who is total, mysterious, and undifferentiated and who at one and the same time transcends and attracts him. But when the believer attempts to speak about his faith and to express his experience of the Absolute, he has to draw on the relative for his terms. He borrows words and images from the culture of his times and milieu. If he wishes to name, systematize, rationalize and legitimatize his experience, he has recourse to the images, concepts and systems of thought connected with a particular culture.

In the same measure in which cultures differ from one milieu to another and from one period to another, it is inevitable that the expression of faith will differ and even give rise to tensions. But is this to say that faith taken in itself is as different as the cultures which give expression to it? Here we need to distinguish between faith and theology, belief and doctrine.

Dialogue between Christian and Muslim "experts" often moves on a theological plane, seemingly unmindful of belief in what lies deepest: the act of faith itself. In affirming that our theologies differ, we automatically suppose that at their source there lies a different faith. Against this backdrop we evaluate the distance which separates Muslim and Christian positions. On both sides it is taken for granted that the gap should be closed by "the other side." We believe that for the sake of honesty and fidelity we cannot change anything in our own faith, even to accommodate the other. At the same time we attempt more or less subtly to persuade the other to change his manner of belief. We allege that truth cannot be negotiated. But in fact, what "truth" are we speaking of? The doctrine of theologians or the simple faith of believers?

We cannot deny that there are differences between the Bible and the Quran; we have already mentioned a number of them. But we also have to recognize that these differences have been greatly magnified by teachings stemming from historical and political factors as much as from scriptural differences. For example, among Christians of the first centuries the doctrine of the Trinity only emerged with great difficulty, and at the price of confrontations between the languages and cultures through which the new faith was trying to express itself. In the same way the dogma of the Incarnation and belief in the divinity of Jesus were not all that obvious to many early Christians. Mutual understanding was reached only by letting go of misunderstandings. For example, terms such as "person" and "nature" did not have the same meaning for Greeks and Latins. Doctrinal negotiations and political intrigues were so closely interwoven that schisms habitually followed the same lines of division as the socio-political areas of influence.

For Muslims as for Christians, formulations of dogma and doctrine were more often the result of polemics and socio-political confrontations than of peaceful and disinterested reflection on the content of Quran or Bible. Driven to respond to the attacks of Christian theologians, the adepts of the young religion which Islam then was had recourse to the same tool as their adversaries, that is to say, Greek thought. Obliged to choose between "essence" and "existence," between "substance" and "accidents," between "nature" and "attributes," in order to describe in simple images what the Quran told them of Allah, Muslim theologians had to make choices which froze the fluid and ambivalent categories of the Quran into rigid and univocal dogmas.

This is how, for example, "the beautiful names of Allah" became Allah's "attributes." In speaking of Allah, the Quran uses descriptive phrases such as "the compassionate one," "he who shows mercy," etc. The devotion of the early Muslims numbered ninety-nine of these descriptive phrases and called them "the beautiful names of Allah."[7] In the view of the Quran these terms made no claim to be "definitions" of Allah, enclosing him within the watertight categories of a philosophical system. They resembled, rather, the touches of an impressionist painting, which suggest fluid contours within a whole centered around the luminosity of the colors rather than precision of lines.

The recitation of these "beautiful names" would rapidly become means of feeding meditation and evoking the physiognomy of Allah in terms at once simple, meaningful, and accessible to all believers. In changing these "beautiful names"

---

[7] In a recent work in which she examines the power of the Islamic religion in forming political and cultural ideologies in several Middle Eastern countries, Judith Miller May draws her inspiration from the Quran but applies its concepts in a way which has generated some controversy (*God Has Ninety-Nine Names*, New York: Simon & Schuster, 1995).

into the "attributes" of Allah, the theological dialectic started up a chain reaction and became involved in a labyrinth of dilemmas which were logically insoluble. Were the "attributes" of Allah distinct from his "essence"? Whether one answered yes or no, one became involved in a series of questions at the end of which one might find some shield with which to defend oneself from external attacks—but what interior progress did one make? In any case one was very far from the categories of the Quran and from the understanding of it enjoyed by the mass of simple believers.

For Muslim and Christian theologians alike, the thought of the Greek philosophers proved to be a fairly adequate tool for scrutinizing a revelation which had appeared in the setting of Semitic thought, thought which found expression in images, metaphors, and stories rather than in watertight concepts built into a rigid system which locked reality in under the pretext of defining it. The understanding of the Quran, as of the Bible, flowed from poetry rather than philosophy, from literary genres rather than systems of thought. At the level of the act of faith, believing Christians and Muslims were closer to each other than were the doctrinal "experts."

Politics and religion

If we wish to reestablish some proportion between what unites Christians and Moslems and what divides them, in the matter of their traditional religious patrimony, another element needs to be considered. It is the relationship between politics and religion, or more precisely, between socio-political situations and theological formulations.

Generally speaking, the great religions require of their followers that they model their actions and societal structures on their religious beliefs. It cannot be denied that this ideal contributed to the progress of civilization and staved off barbarity both in the Christianity of the Middle Ages and in the medieval Muslim world.

But it must also be recognized that things do not always work this way. The believer can attempt to shape society according to his beliefs, but historically the reverse often happens. In adjusting to surrounding circumstances, doctrines are shaped by a social or political situation which they have in some sense legitimized by linking it with some sacred writing. In Christianity as much as in Islam, many schisms can be seen as the result and justification, at the religious level, of ethnic or political tensions and divisions.

For example in Islam, *shî'ism*, a minority branch of Islam, was originally a political party, the "party (*shî'a*) of Ali." Its members held that Ali, because he was the husband of Fatima, the Prophet's daughter, and the father of the Prophet's grandsons, was the only person entitled to be the caliph, that is, the successor of Muhammad as head of the Muslim community. The partisans of Ali, having been defeated in the first armed confrontation with Muslim believers, were forced to take refuge first in Iraq, then in Iran.

The death of Ali, followed by that of his son Hussain at the hands of the troops of the new caliph, did not succeed in discouraging the partisans. Defeated on the political level, they tried to give meaning to their situation by introducing a theological significance. Often oppressed by the majority, the political minority of the partisans of Ali transformed themselves into a dissident religious group. While remaining attached to the Quran and to the teachings and religious practices of the majority of believers, the shi'ites developed doctrines special to them: belief in the hidden Imam (the last descendant of Ali), the redemptive value of suffering and martyrdom, and the return of Imam who would reestablish justice on earth. In the eyes of these "losers," what could be more comforting than the thought that the triumph of the forces of evil and darkness was only apparent and temporary. Invisible to the eyes of the world, Imam mysteriously but truly assured their survival and redemption. United to Imam's suffering, the suffering of believers was progressively driving back the darkness, until the day when the return of Imam would come to consecrate the definitive victory of light and goodness.

We cannot help note the strange affinity between this type of teaching and the condition of the Iranian Muslims of this period. Even if they were converted to Islam, the religion of their Arabian conquerors, these heirs to the dualist philosophy (light/darkness) of ancient Persia were often treated like second class citizens. It is not surprising that they joined the Arab shi'ites, victims like themselves of the ruling Arab class, to express at the doctrinal level their socio-political situation.

In the same way, a glance at "the schism between the Eastern and Western Churches," or at the rise of the Church of England, points to the same conclusion. Doctrinal differences between believers of different confessions are more the result of historical accidents than the logical and necessary consequences of religious faith. Seen from this viewpoint the divergences between Christians and Muslims should be seen as relative and contingent rather than absolute and necessary. These divergences are real, but they are not the whole of reality; they may perhaps not be the most important part of reality.

But overt important

When the Christian says, "I believe in one God," and the Muslim says, "There is no other god than Allah," they are saying one and the same thing. They are expressing in the fewest possible words the very heart of their faith and religious experience. The remainder of their profession of faith reveals the way in which this God manifests himself to them through historical and cultural contexts which may indeed differ from one another.

The imaged or conceptual representations of this God which are formed by believers may differ, but that need not cause us to lose sight of the religious experience they have in common. From this perspective, doctrinal differences between Christians and Muslims, however real, appear less important than what the two share. The differences continue to exist but the proportions we attribute to them become less considerable, and cannot justify doctrinal polemics or armed confrontations.

The Patrimony of
Culture and Civilization

A black hole in our history

Doctrinal differences and military confrontations have never prevented Christians and Muslims from exchanging their creations and inventions on the scientific and technological levels. In this regard, as we have already said, nothing would be more mistaken than to imagine that there has been only confrontation in the relationship between Christians and Muslims. We are often tempted to project the shadow of the present onto the past. Believing that we can discover in the past situations similar to those in our own day, we salve our consciences by blaming the present on the past, convincing ourselves finally that present tensions are the inevitable and fatal consequences of past conflicts. If Christians and Muslims have been enemies from time immemorial, we think, how can things be any different today? This kind of reasoning may be convenient, but it sacrifices a whole sector of reality: Christians and Muslims together have written important pages in the history of Western, if not of world, civilization.

At the first appearance of Islam in the 7th century after Jesus Christ, the Byzantine Empire, heir of the Roman Empire, was in a state of total decadence and Europe was becoming an easy prey to hordes of barbarian tribes. It was the beginning of what has come to be called "the dark period of the Middle Ages." If we believe history books, we easily assent to the impression that after having risen to considerable heights with the Greeks and Romans, the development of Western civilization came to an abrupt halt with the fall of Rome in the 5th century, not to be revived until the Renaissance in about the 14th century. Between these two events there is a kind of black hole in our history. Yet, the development of civilization was not halted: the fact that things went badly in Europe does not mean that they went badly everywhere.

The torchbearers

Curiously enough, the period of our "great darkness" corresponds quite neatly to the period when the Muslim world knew the growth and culmination of one of the most brilliant civilizations the world has ever known. If we are willing to transcend our often rather ethnocentric concept of history, we will see in this fact more than mere coincidence.

Actually, while Europe was overrun with barbarians, the Muslims, especially the Arabians and Iranians, received the torch of civilization from the Greeks and Romans and held it high. Not only did they keep the torch alight; they stirred up its flame with their own genius and integrated the contributions of such far-flung countries as India and China. It is precisely the role played by Muslim civilization which made possible the European Renaissance. Their civilization is, so to speak, the missing link, the bridge over the black hole in our history. Because of this, the Muslims are an integral part of our history. It might be fairer and less ethnocentric to say that as far as culture and civilization are concerned, there has been something of a merging of our history and theirs.

Since it is impossible to draw up a complete balance sheet of Muslim contributions to civilization here, we will merely give a few examples to illustrate what we have just affirmed. When, toward the end of the Middle Ages, European scholars rediscovered the works of the Greek philosophers, they did not read the original Greek, but used the Arab translations made in the great centers of Islamic culture.[8]

The same was true of the scientific legacy of Greek thinkers. For example, their treatises on mathematics, physics, medicine, and astronomy were translated into Arabic and taught in the Muslim universities where the first European scholars, still novices, went to "do their studies." Building on these foundations and broadening them considerably, Muslim scholars were to make important discoveries and promote considerable advances in science and technology.

Every day, without realizing it, we are the

---

[8] St. Thomas Aquinas (1225-1274), the greatest theologian of the West, was very well versed in the works of the Arab philosopher Averroes (1126-1198), for example, and had a good knowledge of Islam. He even wrote two books to help promote dialogue with non-Christians, and with Muslims in particular. One is *Summa Contra Gentiles* and the other *De Rationibus Fidei Contra Saracenos, Graecos et Armenos*. The first book was written to explain the truths of the Catholic faith. The contents are not polemical and non-Christians are not under attack. The second book was written to answer some objections raised by Muslims in their polemics against Christianity. St. Thomas quoted these objections and answered them one by one in ten articles, two of which define the right approach to dialogue. The books of St. Thomas are based on the assumption that Christians and people of other faiths can meet in depth because they have in common the same need for truth and the same ability to grasp it.

beneficiaries of Muslim contributions to civilization. The numerals we use in preference to the clumsy Roman ones are the "Arabic numerals" which the Muslims themselves borrowed from the Indians. Words beginning with *al-* often indicate a Muslim connection. For example, "al-chemy" should remind us that it was the Muslims who invented chemistry, and "al-cohol," the art of distilling.

Even the Crusades provided opportunities for Europeans to bring home Muslim ideas and institutions which they fancied. Thus hospitals, first originating in Muslim Iran, were later to be found in Europe. The same was true of pharmacies. Paper, invented in China, was transmitted to Europe by way of the Muslims.

We could multiply such examples, to the point where we might wonder if those Muslims are entirely mistaken who maintain that in appropriating modern science and technology they are in reality only taking back a heritage which is theirs as well as ours. This leads us to take a look, now, at relations between Christians and Muslims in the context of the modern world.

The Challenges
of the Modern World

The irony and pitfalls of history

Torchbearers of medieval civilization, the Muslims paved the way for the European Renaissance. Consider the irony of history: by the end of this Renaissance, Europeans had not only made up for lost time, but at the dawn of the modern era they had clearly surpassed Muslim civilization. The latter, after having been the fore-runner of medieval development, knew a marked decline. During this time Europeans were making enormous scientific and technological progress. Simultaneously the intellectual and socio-political evolution of Western societies was to lead them to redefine the relationships between science and faith, politics and religion.

Profiting by the decline of the Muslim empires, the great European powers gradually gained control of most Muslim territories and undertook to bring them up to date with Europe and to become, willy-nilly, a part of the modern era.

It is not my purpose here to analyze the

causes of the internal decline of medieval Islam, nor to describe the historical course of Western colonialism. Rather, I shall try to point out the effects of this modern history on Muslim and Christian relations.

From the start it is important to note two pitfalls which have contributed to a prevalent idea of the history of Islam in our day. The first pitfall into which Westerners stumble consists in under-estimating Islam's potential. We are often tempted to consider the modern period of Islam as being essentially the history of the impact of Western progress on a Muslim society perceived as one great passive mass, allergic to progress.

This concept overlooks the fact that even before the intervention of Europeans on Muslim territory, reform movements had been initiated in the very heart of Islam. Whether in Arabia, North Africa, or India, the vigor of these movements indicates that the Muslim community contained within itself forces for self-assessment and renewal.

These forces had been partially shelved by colonial intervention, and partially diverted by the struggle for national independence. But they seem to have surfaced effectively in the heart of the "Islamic renewal" of recent years, to the great surprise of Westerners who believed that Islam had been confined to the mosque and was soon to be relegated to the museum.

As for the idea that Islam or the Muslims are allergic to progress, we may well wonder whether their allergy is to progress itself or to the manner in which this progress is presented to them nowadays. I shall take up this point later.

The second pitfall which, in a way, is the reverse of the first, is to be simplistic in regard to the Muslims, overestimating the role of the West in the modern history of Islam. We might think, for example, that European colonialism, and the West in general, is responsible for all the difficulties Islam may have known in the modern era.

Here again, awareness of the existence of reform movements prior to the coming of the colonists helps to reestablish perspective. If these movements appeared in the four corners of the Muslim world, it was because the latter was not doing too well. This observation challenges the somewhat idealistic view of certain Muslims regarding Islam's past. For them, it was the intervention of Europeans which caused the decline of Islam, and not the reverse. In order to reinstate things, they believe it would suffice to get rid of European influence and regain the glory of medieval Islam.

This idea is both opportunistic and dangerous. Throwing all the blame on others dispenses us from the effort of self-criticism. By the same token it sidesteps the real problems which the reform movements revealed at the very heart of Islam as she had been at the end of the Middle Ages. How can solutions be found for problems we refuse to recognize? We shall return to this question later, demonstrating its political elements.

These two pitfalls are obviously not the only ones encountered in the relations between Muslims and Christians in the modern world. In their manner of relating to modernity, Islam and Christianity have much in common. But here again, what distinguishes them is often advanced in preference to what brings them together. This is what we shall now try to bring out in examining the modern relationships between science and religious belief and between politics and religion.

The impact of modernity: science and faith

In the early sixties I spent three years in Bangladesh, then East Pakistan. One day while waiting for a ferry, a moulvi (Muslim religious leader) addressed me more or less like this:

Look at those students handing out Communist propaganda!... You're a Christian, aren't you? And I'm a Muslim. Compared with these young people we're on the same side because we both believe in God. We're both believers, while today a good number of Muslims and Christians don't believe in anything. In the name of the God they believe in, the Muslims and Christians who do believe ought to join together, instead of sniping at one another...

My friend's remarks were not about a new crusade in which believing Christians and Muslims, faced with a common enemy, would find themselves side by side crossing swords with unbelievers. It was rather a question of solidarity, a sense of community between people who recognized that they had something important in common. His remarks gave me a better perspective. In the Middle Ages what distinguished people from each other was primarily that they belonged to one religion rather than another. In general, people who opposed a religious group belonged to some other religious group. Religious differences thus became major distinctive notes of individual and collective identity. They could also confer a kind of legitimacy upon doctrinal or military confrontations. In this context the perception of a patrimony common to Christians and Muslims, consisting in the fact of belief, would be the background of relationships between Christians and Muslims.

In our day things have changed. In the case brought against religious belief by science and modern thought, believers, whatever their confessional allegiance, find themselves aligned in the dock. Various schools of thought have passed judgment on religion. These may seem cursory to us today, but they have marked believers, giving them notice to examine their faith closely in the light of the criteria of the human or natural sciences.

Thus some take it for granted that scientific laws inherent in nature are sufficient to explain all phenomena. What has not yet been explained today will be tomorrow; it is only a question of time. From this point of view religion would correspond to a kind of stage of mythical and magic thought in the history of humanity. Not being able to find a rational explanation for the origin of the world and other phenomena and events, a creator god was dreamed up who directed history according to his good pleasure. Rites were used in an attempt to persuade the divine power to act benefi-cently upon nature.

In the euphoria introduced by modern scien-tific discoveries and increasing control over natural forces, it was tempting to think that man had no real need of this god he had fabricated in his ignorance, in the days when he had sought answers to questions now resolved by science and technol-ogy.

For others, religion was "the opium of the people." In order to prevent the poorer classes from revolt, the upper classes fostered the idea that the current state of society was willed by God and that privations endured here below would be gener-ously compensated by eternal happiness in heaven. Thus seen, religion became an obstacle to the liberation of the proletariat and to their gaining power. It was a kind of alienation, an evasion which must be neutralized in order that people might gain access to the reality of society.

We could give other examples of cases brought against religion. But what is important for our purpose is to note that in most cases Christian-ity and Islam have received almost the same treat-ment. Since the concept of religion has been globalized, little difference has been recognized between the various religious traditions.

In some instances, however, Islam has been the object of special "treatment" which has restored the medieval arsenal of prejudice against it. In the view of some, Islam is merely an acute case of the pathological phenomenon of religious belief, and Muhammad one more example of what the "cult of heroes" can effect among the masses — blind faith in a mythical person.

Another prejudice has insinuated itself under cover of the study of comparative religions. Noting the pitiable condition and regression of Muslim societies, experts have found a clear explanation: if Muslims are generally inferior in relation to the West, it is because Islam is "an inferior religion," avoiding contact with science and progress and favoring obscurantism. As long as Islamic influence is not neutralized, Muslims will remain inferior. Such prejudices entertained by Europeans can only arouse mistrust and resentment in regard to Muslims.

With the passage of time it may be that for Muslims the major difficulties in relating to modern Western civilization will stem not from the fact that the West is Christian, but rather from the fact that it is Christian no more. In the Middle Ages it was not practical to confront the Christian polemic; Christians remained within the circle of believers. In the modern period, on the other hand, criticism of religion and anti-religious positions are more radical, and the conflict is being carried beyond the circle of believers. Christians and Muslims alike are being forced to take a stand in relation to a whole series of values which at first sight appear to be not only outside the orbit of religious belief but even in contradiction to religion itself.

Christian and Muslim believers alike have had to convince themselves gradually, each group for itself, that some adjustments between modern ideas and religious faith are possible. Among them there can be found minds open to the progress of science, which see it not as a threat but as a means of attaining a more enlightened understanding of their own religious tradition and of adjusting their way of life to modern conditions.

Among both Christians and Muslims these adjustments have caused tensions and confrontations which, even today, divide both communities. "Traditionalists" and "progressives" are found in both religions. Again, dividing lines have shifted. Believers align themselves more according to their way of conceiving religion than their confessional allegiance. We often get the impression that progressives of one religion feel more affinity with progressives in the other than with traditionalists in their own group. Thus we can speak in terms of kinship of spirit and outlook rather than of religious families.

The chief point where these dividing lines appear is the manner of understanding and interpreting the Sacred Scriptures, the Bible and the Quran. Up to the present day many Christians and Muslims shared the same approach in this regard. The sacred books had been written word for word under divine inspiration. God Himself was their Author and the prophet or sacred writer was only the quasi-mechanical transmitter of a message over which he had no control.

This meant, therefore, that these texts were exempt from all error. God could deceive neither Himself nor us. The very words had been chosen by God. One could not make them mean anything other than what they literally said. A man might "comment" on the text, but would never have dared to say he "interpreted" it. If there seemed to be contradictions between certain passages, an explanation was sought. Failing that, one submitted to the mystery of God which surpasses human understanding: *Allahou a'lamou* ("Allah knows best") was the usual conclusion of the most learned treatises of Muslim scholars.

With the advent of modern studies and insights, the sacred texts have been subjected to a rude testing. Their content has been confronted with the discoveries of science, which in turn were based on empirical data verifiable by human reason and not on an act of faith which seemed to evade reason.

Among believers, both Muslim and Christian, many people were convinced of the validity of modern science as well as the truth of Scriptures. For these there seemed no contradiction between faith and reason, since God was the author of nature and its laws as well as the author of the Scriptures. Rightly understood, the Scriptures could not contradict science.

This fundamental conviction led believers to revise their concept and understanding of the Scriptures. They came to distinguish different areas or levels at which science and revelation operated. Thus, Sacred Scriptures were not historical, philosophical, or scientific treatises. Addressed to people of a given era and in terms these people could understand, the Bible or Quran used the categories and images of this era but without necessarily validating them in the name of God. The "truth" which they taught is of a totally different order. It concerns the destiny of human beings beyond time and space, and teaches what must be known and done in order to attain this destiny. When human reason studies the sacred writings it is in order to discover this kind of truth, not those truths which it can discover for itself by studying nature.

This approach has not attracted all believers in Islam; nor has it done so in Christianity either. Those who hold positions of this type, which have often been lumped together under the term "modernism," have frequently been the object of suspicion and condemnation by their religious authorities. Denounced as unbelievers or unfaithful, they have had to defend themselves and to try to convince the authorities that they have no desire to destroy religion but indeed rather to restore its vitality and reaffirm its relevance. In order to do this, they draw from the sources made available by the knowledge of their times. In this, they are but continuing the work of some very highly respected Christian and Muslim theologians of the Middle Ages.

In connection with the understanding of the Scriptures, we cannot pass over in silence a particular point which divides Christians among themselves and which deepens the mistrust of many Muslims in regard to Christianity and the West. I refer to the so-called "historical-critical" method and that of "literary forms," used by Western scholars in their study of the Bible.

Making use of history, archeology, philology, and literary studies, these methods propose to extract the meaning of a text by situating it in its historical context, tracing its author, comparing the redactional elements, and determining its literary genre. In this way they seek the meaning which the text had at the moment when it first reached those for whom it was destined. This meaning can then be transposed to fit our modern historical context and today's readers, that is, believers who want to understand what God is saying to them now through this text.

Among specialists who carry on a Christian-Muslim dialogue, it is often remarked that it is this approach to the sacred text which has caused the widest breach between the two religions. It is felt that the approach has been adopted by Christians, while Muslims as a whole reject it, and that as long as Muslims refuse to study the Quran from this perspective they will not be able to come close to Christians, and will experience even greater difficulty in adapting to the modern world.

This viewpoint has the merit of pointing out clearly and simply a condition for dialogue. But I do not think the actual reality is all that simple, as will be seen if we examine the two affirmations mentioned above at closer range: that historical-critical methods have been adopted by Christians, and rejected by Muslims.

Among Roman Catholic Christians the approach to Scripture of which we have been speaking has long been the object of criticism because it adopts, "more or less overtly, the thesis of the one single meaning [of a text]... and limits the meaning of texts by tying them too rigidly to precise historical circumstances."[9] And while Pius XII in his encyclical *Divino Afflante Spiritu* (1943) insisted that "it is absolutely necessary for the interpreter to go back in spirit to those remote centuries of the East and to make proper use of the help given by history, archaeology, ethnology and other sciences, in order to discover what literary forms the writers of those early ages intended to use and did in fact use," the role of Tradition in the interpretation of the Scriptures remains for Catholics the ultimate norm.

For some in the scholarly community this smacks of an example of legitimacy in principle,

---

[9] Pontifical Biblical Commission: *The Interpretation of the Bible in the Church*, 1993.

but not necessarily in practice. On the one hand, many documents emanating from the Vatican in recent years continue to base themselves on a rather literal interpretation of biblical texts. On the other hand, should a scholar use the historical-critical and literary approaches, or some other modern method, and come up with results not in complete conformity with the official understanding of the text, he runs the risk of denunciation by groups of believers, or more or less direct condemnation by the official authorities. At times his career in teaching and research may even be jeopardized.

It is not only in the Catholic Church that resistance to the use of these methods is observable. Other Churches are also divided. And still others, such as the Pentecostals for example, definitively reject this type of approach altogether.

On the broader horizon, we can easily see in the present development of Muslim fundamentalism a similar sign of the tension accompanying the interpretation of the sacred texts. Fundamentalism, generally based on a literal interpretation of the texts, does not affect Islam alone. It is a worldwide phenomenon and appears in most religious traditions including Christianity. There seems to be a dividing line within it, at the very heart of each religion, between a tendency to interpret the sacred texts in a literal way and a tendency to interpret them within an historical context. The latter tendency has certainly been pushed very far by scholars within Christianity, but this is not to say that it always attracts the majority of believers. We cannot say unequivocally that it has been accepted by all Christians.

As to whether the scriptural approach we are speaking of is rejected by Muslims, there too a considerable nuancing is called for. It is true, however, that most attempts made by Muslim scholars to apply modern methods of interpretation explicitly to the Quran have met with massive resistance, to put it mildly, on the part of their religious authorities. The resistance flows from many causes, some of which may likewise be observed among Christians.

In the first place, this approach is based on the assumption that we may examine a sacred text in the same way we would a human production. This premise cannot stand, in view of the faith of people who believe that the Quran, or the Bible, is not a human production, but is entirely the work of God, a work which should neither be "reconstituted" nor "criticized" by any human being, regardless of the extent of his learning.

For Muslims the factor of mistrust compounds this. These methods of approaching Scripture were invented by Europeans, like many of the institutions which colonialism imposed on Muslims and which dislocated Muslim society. They have seen the considerable damage done by them to Christianity, causing many believers to lose their faith in God and their reverence for Jesus.

Certain Muslim polemicists find in the works of Christian exegetes an unhoped-for weapon for demonstrating the justice of the Quran when it affirms that Christians have falsified their Scriptures or misused them. But for the most part Muslims have difficulty understanding the casual manner in which Jesus, whom they venerate as a great prophet but not as God, can be treated, in movies for example, by Christians and in the presence of Christians who in principle consider him to be God. For some of them, this is a clear indication that one should avoid like the plague methods of interpretation and concepts of revelation advanced by Christian exegetes.

Resistance to modern methods of biblical exegesis has not prevented a good number of Muslims from working out adjustments between their understanding of the Quran and modern life. Without borrowing European methods of biblical interpretation, Muslim modernists, particularly in India, have drawn from the Quran and from the teachings of the Prophet elements which seem to harmonize with the values of the modern world. Like many Christian believers in this respect, they have in some sort "projected" onto the sacred writings the essentials of their own convictions in their present situation. Through this very subtle and often unconscious procedure they have succeeded in convincing many Muslims that modern values are neither foreign to them nor alienating, since they can be found in the Quran and in the sayings of the Prophet. This "rereading" of the Quran and the Prophet has allowed them to legitimize, at least initially, the enterprise of the modernization of Muslim society.

The fact that fundamentalist movements seem to enjoy considerable prominence in Islam today should not cause us to forget that Muslim modernists have had and still have considerable influence among Muslim believers. Their influence does not necessarily take the form of a movement or political party; it consists rather in a mindset, a more or less conscious instinct by which many Muslims, while maintaining their faith allegiance to the Quran and the Prophet, situate the Quran and the Prophet's action in the historical context of an era, and distance themselves from a purely literal understanding of the text. They thus find in the Quran and the life of the Prophet motives for advancing in the modern world. The rejection of explicit use of Western methods of exegesis does not mean, therefore, that Muslims reject the entire evolution in their practical understanding of the Quran.

Thus, prescinding from the circle of "experts," it is not certain that Christians and Muslims taken as a whole are all that far apart in the matter of interpreting Sacred Scripture. What I have tried to establish above suggests rather that the generality of Christians do not accept as widely as might be thought the methods of modern exegesis, while the generality of Muslims accept in practice more adjustments in their understanding of the Quran than the official attitude of religious leaders toward Muslim modernists would indicate. In concluding this section of my exposition, I should mention that the work of Western scholars has not had exclusively negative consequences for the relationship between Christians and Muslims. Quite the contrary. If some scholars give the impression of having scrutinized Islam the better to refute it, others — and they are at least as numerous — have approached the study of Islam in a more objective and serene manner, and have contributed greatly to correcting the biassed image which Westerners often have of Islam.[10] They have sometimes led Muslims themselves to rediscover certain elements of their religious and cultural patrimony.

We can think, for example, of the renewal of interest in Islamic mysticism, philosophy, and theology. Some Western scholars have devoted their lives to publishing, translating, and commenting on the works of the great medieval Muslim thinkers.[11] Muslim art, too, has aroused the interest and enthusiasm of Western scholars, who have made inventories of architectural and ornamental masterpieces which are considered to be a part of the artistic patrimony of humanity, and made them known to the public.[12]

These scholars have been and still are bridges between Muslims and the West. In making Islam

---

[10] For example, to mention only a few: Louis Gardet, Régis Blachère, Maxime Rodinson, Denise Masson, Francesco Gabrielli, William Montgomery Watt, H.A.R. Gibb, Bernard Lewis, Norman Daniel, G.E. von Grunebaum, Wilfred Cantwell Smith, Charles J. Adams.

[11] For example, research scholars such as Louis Massignon, Henri Corbin, G.-C. Anawati, Eva Meyerovitch, A.J. Arberry, R.A. Nicholson, R.J. MacCarthy, Hermann Landolt.

[12] For example, G. Marçais, K.A.C. Creswell, R. Ettinghausen, G. Wiet.

better known they have contributed to the lessen-
ing of the prejudices which weighed upon the
relationship between Christians and Muslims. They
have helped Christians to understand that Islam is
highly deserving of their interest, and have shown
Muslims that Westerners are capable of understanding and appreciating something of Islam.

This scholarly activity and contact with
Muslims has led a good number of Christians to
throw off medieval prejudices and challenge their
own theological positions. Today some sincerely
believe that the Quran is "a true revelation" and
Muhammad an authentic prophet.

Without going that far, the Vatican has
adopted a very positive attitude toward Islam as
well as the other great religious traditions. In a
spirit of reconciliation, the Holy See maintains
ongoing relations with various Muslim organiza-
tions. Dialogue with Islam took a new turn in the
work and in the texts of the Second Vatican Council (1962-65) where the rediscovered dimension of
Christianity as the People of God marching to-
wards salvation in obedience to the universal call of
God to unity, led the Church to an attitude of
humility and open-hearted acceptance of others.
Thus the document *Lumen Gentium* states: "The plan
of salvation also includes those who acknowledge

the Creator. In the first place among these are the Muslims, who, professing to hold the faith of Abraham along with us, adore the one merciful God, who on the last day will judge mankind." In the second chapter of the Vatican II document *Nostra Aetate* Christians are urged to enter into sincere dialogue with Muslims. This will help to create mutual understanding at the doctrinal as well as at the social level. This document urges all sides to wipe out misunderstandings and to build a new world where justice and peace can find their full realization. There is also an appeal to forget the clashes of the past: "Although in the course of the centuries many quarrels and dissensions have arisen between Christians and Muslims, this most sacred Synod now pleads with all to forget the past and urges that a sincere effort be made to strive for mutual understanding."[13]

The Secretariat for Non-Christians (recently renamed the Pontifical Council for Inter-Religious Dialogue) was established by Pope Paul VI on May

---

[13] *Lumen Gentium* (Dogmatic Constitution on the Church, Nov. 21, 1964), par. 16, p. 367 and *Nostra Aetate* (Declaration on the Relation of the Church to Non-Christian Religions, Oct. 28, 1965), par. 3, p. 740 in *Vatican Council II: The Conciliar and Post Conciliar Documents*, Revised Edition, edited by Austin Flannery, O.P. (Boston: St. Paul Editions, 1988).

19, 1964. This Council has been working for the past thirty some years to promote goodwill, harmony and understanding between believers of different faiths. On October 22, 1974, a Commission for Islam was formed, composed of a group of specialists and consulters. This commission was added to the already existing office for Islam.[14]

The Popes have led the Church in trying to break down the barriers of prejudice inherited from the past. Addressing the Mufti of Istanbul, Fikr Yarus in 1967, Pope Paul VI said: "We must express our esteem for Muslims and, on this basis of common truth, we are called to promote together

---

[14] There have been many Christian-Muslim dialogue conferences all around the world as a result of this Commission's work. To mention a few: Geneva, 1969, Rome, 1970, Bromine, 1972, Ghana, Cairo, Tunis and Rome, 1974, Hong Kong, 1975, Tripoli, 1976, Qurtaba and Beirut, 1977, Cairo, 1978, Geneva and Tunis, 1979, Beirut, 1980, Colombo and Tunis, 1982, Rome and Casablanca, 1985, Tunis, 1986, Multan, 1991 and every year in Windsor Oman from 1984 to 1988. Besides these many more conferences have taken place on national and international levels all around the world. Muslims, too, have made many efforts to promote harmony between Christians and Muslims. The World Muslim Congress always invites Christians to participate and give a message at their meetings and several Muslim universities also invite Christian professors to give lectures. (James Channan, O.P., *Christian-Muslim Dialogue in Pakistan*, Lahore, National Commission for Christian-Muslim Relations, 1995).

social justice, moral values, peace and liberty." In the same spirit Pope John Paul II, during his visit to Ankara in 1979, spoke of "the deep spiritual bonds" that unite Muslims and Christians who have a common faith in God and consequently can live together in a spirit of friendship and peace. The same idea of principles in common, as well as that of mutual respect and service for humanity emerges in all his numerous speeches addressed to the Muslims with whom he has met in Rome, Kenya, France, Germany, the Philippines and Morocco. In his annual message to the Muslim community on the Feast of Ramadan, he always asks that an abundance of God's blessings be poured out upon the Muslim peoples. Other Christian Churches do the same through the World Council of Churches. [15]

The traumas of modernization: politics and religion

The attitude of Christian Churches which we have just noted clearly marks an evolution in the

---

[15] In *Theology Digest* 39:4 (Winter, 1992), pp. 302-320, the excellent article by Thomas Michel, "Christian-Muslim Dialogue in a Changing World," makes the point about the dialogue between Christians and Muslims. I shall return to this a little further on.

undergirding concept of the missionary enterprise. The latter was based — and still is in some cases — on the idea that outside the Christian faith there can be no salvation. If one wishes non-Christians to be saved one must lead them to Christian faith. Responding to this appeal, numerous Christians have devoted their lives to this cause which in itself was a noble one.

Yet basically this concept introduced a relationship of superiority-inferiority between Christians and Muslims. It was in a sense the religious face of the colonial enterprise. In matters religious as well as political, social, educational, legal, and technological, colonialism, in its humanistic and philanthropic thrust, wanted Muslims to profit by the best (read European). For in the eyes of the colonists the best was what they themselves possessed, that which had enabled them to progress so far as to impose their will on the rest of the world.

This philanthropic attitude was not the only note of colonialism, nor its most outstanding feature. In Muslim lands most European colonies were first and foremost colonies of exploitation. If colonists wanted to modernize these territories, it was chiefly because they would contribute to the prosperity of the mother country. Often the rhythm of changes imposed on colonized societies corresponded more to the needs of the mother country's metropolis than to the local population's capacity for absorption.

Some Christian believers undertook the defense of the colonized peoples and opposed the abuses of their own countries. But in general the Christian Churches had more positive relationships with the colonial powers than with the State in their mother countries. By more or less tacit agreement, the establishment and maintenance of schools, clinics and hospitals were entrusted to the Churches.

The connection between politics and religion in the colonial enterprise still weighed heavily upon the relationships between Christians and Muslims. First, the case against colonialism included Christianity: the colonizers came from Christian countries, and Christian Churches ranged themselves on the side of power.

As a result, if Muslims were ready to recognize the humanitarian dedication shown by the missionaries and their contribution to the improvement of local populations, they questioned the motives behind this dedication. Too often they had the impression that the missionaries were not simply interested in them as persons, but wanted to convert them. Even today, vast projects of humanitarian aid are more or less overtly associated with enterprises of conversion, for the profit of Christian groups.

In a more global sense, Muslim mistrust and resentment of the West mark the modernization and secularization which the colonial era has left as a heritage in Muslim countries.

To begin with I should like to dissipate an ambiguity connected with a current prejudice against Islam and Muslims. Many people, as I have already noted, think that Islam is allergic to modernity and that Muslims resist change and progress. It may be useful to recall that in past centuries Muslims were in the vanguard of progress and civilization and introduced innovations in all sectors of daily life. They gave proof of remarkable openness and creativity in integrating elements borrowed from various cultures.

In the modern period the situation is different, owing particularly to political and psychological circumstances. In the early days of Islam the first Muslims, coming from Arabia, did not have a highly developed cultural and social code. As they absorbed whatever they encountered in their travels, they did not have the feeling that they were sacrificing the considerable cultural heritage left them by their ancestors. In fact, by reason of their dominant political situation they themselves were making decisions based on what they considered to be to their own advantage. Thus they gradually developed institutions corresponding to their own scale of values and, less ideally, to their beliefs. When the colonists undertook to modernize Muslim societies the Muslims were no longer their own masters. Now it was not they, but the colonial powers, who decided what was good for them, and imposed it, often in a very cavalier fashion. Furthermore, in order to make room for the European influx, the Muslims habitually had to scrap their own institutions and give up what had constituted the success and happiness of their ancestors through the centuries.

One can easily understand that, presented in this way, "progress" and modernization, while at the same time seductive, have been fairly traumatic for Muslims. Add to this the sequels to modernization and it will be equally clear how most Muslims feel today about things coming from the West. Actually, modernization, which seemed to have succeeded so well in the West, has not been so profitable for Muslim countries. I believe the chief reason for this is precisely that the kind of modern progress realized in Europe and America has been achieved largely at the expense of the colonized countries, among others those producing oil, especially Muslim countries. Oil, for example, is transported from the Gulf at ridiculous prices, lower than the cost would be from local sources. In this way Europe and America, while preserving their own resources, have known a rapid industrialization and development at a relatively low cost.

During this same period of time colonized countries have known a mitigated development and have seen their socio-cultural fabric disintegrate as a result of the invasion of Western culture and institutions. Having inherited power at the departure of the colonials, the Westernized elite, who had been in the avant-garde in the struggle for independence, have gradually grown apart from the masses, withdrawn and concerned for their own profit. Is it any wonder that today many Muslims retain only the dark side of the colonial heritage? This heritage often constitutes a barrier in relationships between Christians and Muslims. The barrier does not separate religions; rather, it divides those who think they have been exploited from those who prefer not to ask themselves whether they have been exploited or not.

Another point which seems to separate Muslims and Christians is the question of secularization. In the West secularization has been a gradual process whereby Church and state have been separated, each being assigned a well-defined domain: temporal concerns pertain to the state, spiritual concerns to the Church. From this point of view — not shared by all Christians — religion becomes a private matter which need not interfere with public affairs. Having reached "maturity," in the eyes of the secularists, humanity has no further need of religious tutelage from on high. The state is responsible for the destiny of citizens in this world, while religion assures its devotees a destiny beyond. Religion is no longer the center of gravity and identity for society. This is not to say that no one believes in God and in the afterlife, but rather that it is no longer beliefs that define society's values.

At first sight this concept is diametrically opposed to that of Islam, which is, at one and the same time, *dîn wa dawla*, religion *and* society, religion *and* the state. Here again our view must be nuanced in opposing theoretical formulations. We should regard them not merely in themselves but in view of the respective practices of the two collectivities, Christian and Muslim.

Among Christians the "secular city" is less secular than it was a few decades ago. After having made laicism (systematized secularism) an indisputable absolute imposed on all civilized society, accommodations have gradually been admitted. Real life cannot be departmentalized as easily as ideas. Secular authorities are often the first to break the rules and refer to religion in the marketplace. In doing this they perhaps reflect the evolution of mindsets as much as a concern for political advantage, banking on the "return to religion" observable in many Western societies.

Muslims for their part have always practiced a distinction between the political order under caliph or sultan and the religious order under religious leaders. Theoretically, in the state everything is ruled by religion, if one subscribes to the concept of Islamic Law (*shari'a*) which controls the entire life of believers in society and holds the place of legislative power. Executive power is also at the service of religion, as is judiciary power.

A glance at history shows us that there have always been sectors of activity entrusted to tribunals other than those of the *shari'a*, which have functioned practically autonomously and on a parallel with it. Caliphs and other political heads, for their part, were not always the most zealous of believers. While respecting Islam officially they managed to intervene with their own authority, making ordinances and administrative regulations which could have far-reaching results. A large number of political theories elaborated by medieval Muslims demonstrate in reality an attempt to fill in the gap between the principle of Allah's sovereignty and an actual state which was often far from conforming to this principle. In this sense traditional Muslim society tended much more to pragmatism than to dogmatism.

Accustomed for centuries to adjusting principles to practice, Muslims have done much the same thing in the modern era. Acting according to the pragmatic instinct which characterized them in the Middle Ages, they have often adopted Western institutions at a far more rapid pace than theoretical legitimacy could keep up with.

Under cover of a return to Islam, current Islamic movements extol the supreme control of religion over society, under the aegis of the *shari'a*. They are apt to give the impression of wanting to return to the situation which prevailed before the arrival of the colonists. In reality, however, their radical dissatisfaction with the present causes them to project onto the past what they dream of for the future.

In my opinion most Muslims, even those who are dissatisfied with their present condition, do not follow the Islamists in this area. Like most Christian believers, they take up a position between two extremes: state-controlled totalitarianism — the control of the state over the lives of individuals including their religion, and the opposite extreme of religious totalitarianism or religious control over the lives of individuals and over the state.

As to present relations between Christians and Muslims, the mistrust caused by the separation between politics and religion in secularization is less serious than that posed by the confusion between politics and religion which has been brought about by the utilization of religion for political purposes.

At this point, above all since the Iranian revolution in 1979, leaders directing Western politics vie with the heads of Muslim states in referring to God in patriotic discourses. When an armed conflict like the Gulf War occurs (between Iraq and Kuwait), they outdo one another in their attempt to convince the world that it is a religious war, when in reality it is not even a question of a territorial dispute, but rather of control over oil resources.

Political leaders are not the only ones to come up with an explosive religious-political blend. Among Christians, Muslims, and other groups, extremist religious leaders can be found who profit from the slightest incident to fantasize a plot aimed at suppressing their religion. They attempt to spark anger against the supposed authors of the plot, usually members of some other religious group taken as a whole.

It is not always easy for believers, whether Muslims or Christians, to discern what is really at work beneath inflammatory words and demagogic speeches. It is not always easy to know, in a given situation, whether a religious belief which sows fear and hatred has gone off the track partially, or has completely left the orbit of religious affairs. Adequate information is doubtless a valuable asset in identifying the elements of a situation, perceiving what is at stake, and dispelling the smoke screens resulting from the manipulation of religion for political ends. For most believers, the most accessible sources of information are the media: television, radio, newspapers. At first sight the media claim to give solutions, but could it be that they are a part of the problem?

Media information and optical illusions

The profusion of images and information proliferated by the media creates the impression that we are on the spot and know the people. More often than not, however, we are being shown only what will catch our attention with its shock value. The media are much the same the world over. By their very nature they cannot present the whole of reality. Therefore they cut here and there, omit certain things and retain others. What is omitted is the daily, the normal, the ordinary. The assumption is that the obvious in our lives can be of little interest.

On the other hand, on the day that the ordinary man, in a moment of despair, strangles his wife at home or shoots some stranger in the subway, he suddenly becomes "interesting." He makes the papers and the TV. We have to know all about him. His action becomes the lens, the prism through which we scrutinize his life, as if nothing he has done or lived through prior to this has any meaning or interest except insofar as it has built up to this action.

It is the same for groups. When the media, on a global scale, portray horrors which are associated covertly or openly with an ethnic, national, or religious group, these images become the lens through which we view the group. It is as if they said to us, "There! Now you get the picture: this is what Muslims are like... ." As if Islam explained everything in the lives of Muslims, and as if Christianity were responsible for everything in the lives of Christians. In 1979, Edward Said rightly observed:

> "Islam" cannot explain everything in Africa and Asia, any more than Christianity can explain Chile or South America. [...] Wouldn't it allay some of our fears if we accepted the fact that people do the same things inside Islam and outside it, that Muslims are living in history and in our common world, and not just in an Islamic context?[16]

More recently Thomas Michel, a specialist on Islam who directs the Office for Islam on the Pontifical Council for Inter-Religious Dialogue in Rome, stated:

> Some of the most interesting and significant examples of Muslims and Christians living together have not been reported; they rarely interest the newspapers. It is not the fault of jour-

---

[16] Edward W. Said in an article in *Time* (vol. 113, n. 16, April 1979), which gives a synopsis of his book *Orientalism* (New York: Random House, 1979).

nalists or editors. Rather, it is the nature of the news to focus attention on the dramatic, the extraordinary. If, during the last fifty years, Christians and Muslims have lived together in harmony and with mutual benefit in some city in France or some village in Upper Egypt, this is not news. But if a handful of racists burn down a Muslim prayer room in a French city, or if extremists destroy a church in Egypt, it becomes top news.[17]

The author then draws upon hundreds of examples reported to him and gives us a range of facts illustrating what he calls "the dialogue of life." Throughout the world, quietly and without fanfare, unknown groups of Christians and Muslims are working to build up positive relationships at the level of daily life. It is this "dialogue of life" we should count on, as much as the dialogue of the experts, if we are to find a viable future for relations between Christians and Muslims. This synchronizes with what I have tried to establish in the preceding pages, and from which I shall now draw some conclusions.

---

[17] Thomas Michel, *loc. cit.*, p. 315.

Beyond images and doctrine:
a common destiny

In relationships between Christians and Muslims there are a certain number of more or less obvious pitfalls which often create obstacles. Avoiding these pitfalls, Christians and Muslims can approach a basic, common foundation on which to build and carry on profound and lasting relationships.

We could stigmatize under the umbrella term of idolatry the temptations which we encounter on the road to good relations between Christians and Muslims. In their manner of conceiving and entering into a relationship with the divine Absolute, human beings have recourse to the relative, to categories and realities borrowed from their sociocultural environment. In time, through a kind of osmosis, believers more or less consciously come to clothe the divine Absolute with the relative. Created realities which in the beginning had value as means in the service of the divine acquire a kind of value in themselves and conceal what it was their mission to express and represent. In this sense we could say that they become idols.

The first "idols" I would like to speak of in the present context of Christian-Muslim relations are dogmas. Like many realities in human life, doctrines and dogmas are good servants but bad masters. Useful in explaining, systematizing and rationalizing the elements of religious belief, doctrines formulated in the course of the centuries by Christians and Muslims can also come to mask the very essence and object of the act of belief: acquiescence and adherence to a God whom we cannot enclose within the human categories we use to evoke Him. In relationships between believers the conceptual doctrinal approach doubtless has its place; but it should not take up all the space. It should not replace a global, structural approach in which we seek, beyond words and concepts which may differ from each other, a fundamental structure and elements and content which may vary only slightly from one religious tradition to the other. It is not a question here of denying the differences, but of restoring them to the level of the relative, of reestablishing the proportions we give them in relation to what is first, fundamental and common to all believers: the act of believing in the divine, and of perceiving Him as an Absolute, in comparison with Whom everything else, including doctrines and forms of worship, can have only a very relative importance, the importance of a good servant who should not replace or conceal the master.

Another form of idol is the cult of "the holy man," "the man of God." That there should be, among believers, men in whom we recognize a certain authority and a capacity to guide others in seeking and serving God, is a very normal phenomenon among social human beings. But here again, from the moment when we confer on these human beings a quasi-absolute power, they risk becoming idols who turn us away from God rather than to Him. When believers confer on another human being the right to speak in the name of God, and follow his directions blindly, they end by turning him into a kind of god who distances them from the one God and can at the same time set them in conflict with other believers who may range themselves under the banner of some other "holy man," all in the service of the same God.

Believers, whether Christians or Muslims, may also be tempted to confer considerable power on a politician who appeals to their religious feelings. Manipulated by this "strong man," religious affiliation then becomes a factor which crystallizes and legitimizes the political or military struggle against a group belonging to some other religious tradition. In this way the "strong man" comes between believers and their God, and sets some believers against others.

It would be tragic for Muslims and Christians to succumb to the lure of modern idols, allowing their fidelity to the one God to be turned away from the Absolute to the relativity of a culture or a society, by doctrines or human beings.

We cannot deny the usefulness of meetings of specialists or experts in the interests of dialogue, and of negotiations between politicians in search of peace. But in a more fundamental way the challenge presented to the mass of believers consists in transcending images and prejudices so as to perceive themselves first and foremost as men, human beings living in the same global village.

Rabindranath Tagore (1861-1941), the Nobel prize winning Indian poet, has said that love does not consist in looking at one another, but in looking together in the same direction. Christians and Muslims may look at each other, recognizing the need for exchanges and dialogues about their beliefs. But there are limits, sometimes reached very rapidly, to this "conciliatory" approach. Meanwhile the most crying needs of our modern world risk being denied concrete answers.

An economic crisis, a crisis of civilization, the survival of humanity and of the planet, are at stake. Rather than reassess our differences, Christians and Muslims might well become aware of the radical commonality of their destiny as human beings confronted with hitherto unheard of problems.[18]

They might look together in the same direction. This would develop their concern for the well-being of human beings regardless of creed or race. This is not to say that they must set aside their own religious convictions. Quite the contrary, it is precisely their faith which prompts them to take this step. Preoccupation with improving the lot of human beings, not only in the next life but also in this present world, lies at the very heart of the message of the two great religious traditions, Islam and Christianity. By looking together in this direction Muslims and Christians will each see their own identity and dynamism increase as it is joined to a common destiny, that of all humanity.

---

[18] Vatican Council II, as mentioned earlier in the text, had already invited them to do this in 1965 (*Nostra Aetate, op. cit.*): "Although in the course of the centuries many quarrels and dissensions have arisen between Christians and Muslims, this most sacred Synod now pleads with all to forget the past and urges that a sincere effort be made to strive for mutual understanding. On behalf of all mankind, let them make common cause of safeguarding and fostering social justice, moral values, peace, and freedom."

Bibliography

CHANNAN, James, O.P., *Christian-Muslim Dialogue in Pakistan*, Lahore, National Commission for Christian-Muslim Relations, 1995.

DANIEL, Norman, *Islam et Occident*, Paris, Cerf, 1993.

HENTSCH, Thierry, *L'Orient imaginaire*, Paris, Editions de Minuit, 1988.

LONGTON, Joseph, *Fils d'Abraham: panorama des communautés juives, chrétiennes et musulmanes*, Brepols et CIB Maredsous, 1987.

MICHEL, Thomas, "Christian-Muslim Dialogue in a Changing World," *Theology Digest* 39:4 (Winter 1992), pp. 302-320.

RODINSON, Maxime, *La fascination de l'Islam: les étapes du regard occidental sur le monde musulman; les études arabes et islamiques en Europe*, Paris, F. Maspero, 1980.

SAID, Edward W., *Orientalism*, New York, Random House, 1979.

WAARDENBURG, Jean-Jacques, *L'Islam dans le miroir de l'Occident: comment quelques orientalistes occidentaux se sont penchés sur l'Islam et se sont formé une image de cette religion*, Paris, Mouton, 1962.

WATT, W. Montgomery, *Islam and Christianity Today. A Contribution to Dialogue*, London, 1983.

DATE DUE

MAR 3 1 2005			
DEC 0 2 2005			
MAY 03 2006			
APR 1 8 2008			